24 Études

by Kate Clem

/Етюд/ /Etüde/
a special form of Ukrainian poetry writing

Cover design: Liza Medvediuk
(Stuttgart, Germany)

Linocut prints: Oksana Ginchuk
(Kyiv, Ukraine)

ISBN 9783757853839

to those who are forever free...

Introduction: This poetry collection is a study of my feelings

The étude (етюд, Etüde) is a special admired form of writing in Ukrainian poetry practice – it is self-expression and a study of self – an artist observes a scene and expresses the feelings aroused at the moment of encounter with the subject matter – in my case observing myself as I hang on suspended in time and space, in between of all the life changes – all happening in the years when I moved abroad from home.

Ètudes are written in English, Ukrainian and partly German. I consider those études written far away from home not full, not finished forms of representation as my identity started to transform into some form of hybrid identity bubble – do I need to be complete, yes but. How or perhaps... not yet.

What is also not complete is the number 24 –

this is the day of Ukrainian independence in 24.08.1991

this is the day I was born – 24.08.1993

this is the day when my freedom and of Ukraine got violated 24.02.2022

There are more than 24 études in this étude-collection. But 24 is what created me and hurts me the most at the moment.

As long as I step over myself, I cross the time.line of 24. Maybe then. Then it occurs to me that on 25th of August my grandfather was born. Maybe on a 26th. Maybe then. I will be healed. Again.

переклад вступу для мами

Етюд — особлива форма написання в українській поезії — це самовираження та дослідження себе — митець чи мисткиня, що спостерігає сцену та висловлює почуття, що виникають у момент зіткнення з об'єктом — у моєму випадку це моє спостереження за собою, коли я знаходжусь завмерши у часі та просторі, між усіма змінами життя, що відбувалися, коли я переїхала за кордон від рідного дому.

Етюди написані англійською, українською та частково німецькою мовами, відображають гібридний характер ідентичності, який став формуватися всередині мене. Етюди слугують поміркованою репрезентацією моєї постійної трансформації, ставлячи під сумнів поняття цілісності та того, що означає бути цілим.

o   Число 24 має велике значення у цій колекції —
o   Це День Незалежності України: 24 серпня 1991 року
o   Це мій день народження: 24 серпня 1993 року
o   Це день порушення моєї особистої свободи та свободи України: 24 лютого 2022 року

У безлічі присутніх тут етюдів, число 24 виступає розважливим нагадуванням про піки та спади на моєму життєвому шляху. Ця збірка поезій є інтимним дослідженням моїх почуттів, виразним зображенням емоцій та досвідів, що вплинули на мене.

Поки я переступаю через себе, я перетинаю часову лінію числа 24. Можливо 25-го, можливо тоді... Тоді мені згадується, що 25-го серпня народився мій дідусь. Можливо 26-го. Можливо тоді. Я знову буду зціленою.

Then it occurs to me, on a 26th — the Chornobyl Disaster happened

Тоді я згадую, що 26-го – сталася Чорнобильська катастрофа

a study of the étude

Étude is a small, fragmentary work of art that captures a specific moment of an emotional nature. It lacks a specific plot and, through the use of authorial techniques, reproduces the inner state of a personality, evoking a corresponding aesthetic effect in the reader.

Etudes can take many forms in Ukrainian literature, art and music including poetry, painting, music and drama.

They are often highly introspective and reflective, and they may explore themes such as love, loss, grief, or the beauty of nature.

The history of Ukrainian étude varies, depending on how you interpret it. I imagine, it might have been in 1890s, when the writers who were also somewhat painters (so am I), who were repressed by the evil government of a time, who were sent to prisons without any writing equipment – they would make a mental sketch of their feelings on the way to slavery: the rails, the hitting metal, the wagons, the homeland fields, the steppes, the sunflowers, moving away, the nostalgic desire to return – those mind sketches would be written not with pencils but rather with feelings – those writers-painters would memorize it, repeat it like a prayer, while in exile – and when they returned home –

they would write it down and plant it near the nearest cranberry plant – and the mind étude would grow into today and now, and here am I – an étude 2.0, a consumable nostalgic product of what they have planted, available for a global audience.

some instructions how to write the étude:

1. PICK AN OBJECT OF YOUR DESIRE

2. DESCRIBE HOW YOU FEEL ABOUT IT AS IF MAKING A MIND SKETCH

HERE ARE SOME WRITING GUIDELINES:

- KEEP IT SHORT
- USE A LARGE NUMBER OF ARTISTIC DEVICES, METAPHORS, EPITHETS
- CONVEY YOUR FEELINGS, EMOTIONS, IMPRESSIONS
- BE OVERLY DRAMATIC AND ADD TRAGEDY INTO YOUR FEELINGS (I KNOW THAT YOUR WHOLE LIFE YOU WERE TOLD TO KEEP IT TOGETHER — SO LET IT OUT)
- CHOSE ONLY ONE HUGE PROBLEM FOR ONE ÉTUDE AND DESCRIBE IT SHORTLY (AS EVERYBODY ELSE, THE READER OF AN ÉTUDE CANNOT BEAR TOO MANY FEELINGS AT ONCE)
- EMPHASIZE ON A SPECIFIC MOOD, TONE, OR THEME THAT WILL MAKE EVERYONE SUFFER WITH YOU BY DESCRIBING VERY VIVIDLY THE SETTINGS YOU ARE EMOTIONALLY IN.

FOLLOW THE PRACTICE GUIDE IN THE END OF THIS BOOK AND WRITE YOUR OWN ÉTUDE!

Chapter 23

You can call me Kate, Kate Clem. But my real name is Kateryna. Катерина Валеріївна Медведюк

étude about the epilogue

Epilogue could have been
But epilogue is not
the beginning
is the end
either you awoke
and pretend to have a start
or you work remotely from home
and your better self-half
starting over and over
coffee cups in the mornings
while the other has given up
no clue with what to start
and how to end
concluding conclusions
is my special art —
stream of consciousness
epilogue-ing is a
part of
my every second half

étude about who I am

I am highly irritable
When somebody touches me
I am highly un-emotional
When it comes to emotional movies
I am highly in love when
The words are a poem
I am highly depressed when
I am not myself
And what is self if not the poems if not the emotional movies and
endings if not the touches of people you love of people you hate
if not the wounds if not the laughs and memories and core
memory moments if not the broken heart always on its way to a
holy healing

my name reveals about. étude

what about names
do they carry
stereo. types. too?!
what about. mine?!
why. I keep calling
clementine!!!
is it not a hidden
desire
to be — else ...
cry for help
for a once in a lifetime
bohemian style?
in the old days
Kateryna used to be a victim
—

synonym to Ukraïna
now?
not a victim
a style
I hated my name for
a while. me.
myself. but why?
who
needs "bohemian"
anyway — these days
we are all artists
in a various less
bohemian ways
what's your name?

étude to adulthood

My friend asked me:
When is adulthood
Some have seen war some have lived through tragedies and split personalities disorders without being diagnosed by physicians some have never been to doctors because lack of doctors in the healthcare system some have quit jobs because jobs are boring and life is full of adventures and pain —
adventurous pain is what makes adulthood such an adult-looking adult-feeling.
I thought of the question
For a while now
And even though I wish to stay
I wish to stop
I wish —
I have never seen war —
But I wished not to be
Even if I am
I don't want to be
—
So I answered no
I am no adulthood
I am me

étude to the whole world

This world is a sad place
World without illusions
World confused by hardship and
news reports on you tube
This world is a sad place
As an adult you
don't know anything about public
TV subscription
You are too young for being public
Too young for knowing anything about TV
But old enough to worry about the ending of things and enjoying
long movie titles
Eternally   Sunshine
because you treat all the things that are real like real things you
don't dream big you don't want to change you don't want to ask
you keep accepting the pain
You are what reality gives you
You hate to change YouTube videos you replay news reports you
hate advertisement but you kind of like it
you keep changing providers but the problem is
The world is no illusion
for those who are dreamers
Accept it
Or run from yourself
Run towards the voice from inside of you
Tube
Unless You
Tune
In

étude to Peter Breughel the Younger

Peter Breughel the Younger reminds me of communism
and of all sorts of collective activities done to protect
the goods of society

He reminds of extensive work
that relates the people
to their land and to seasons
that turn those people to
Slaves

Of seasons and government
Peter Brueghel doesn't know of communism yet
And his paintings of four seasons are displayed in the museum in
the country where everything reminds of communism and yet
Do you think they thought of that
Un-relative-ly to that they hang the paintings anyway
close to the bloody revolution square

I guess it is an étude

I guess I happened to be free the moment you left me
I guess the pain from that moment on reminds me of you
I guess you are equal to pain
As I am equal to you
I guess we could be still together
But I choose pain every time over freedom
I guess I should have fought for it
But I choose to be alone and now
I order my coffee alone in the eastern city that still reminds me
of you
My freedom land
my painwall
my equal home
that I replaced this year
with loneliness and heartbreak
over multiple minutes
that make up my day

dream étude

I dream

To disappear and dissolve into city
Called Utrecht and start. my new
life
From the new
page I have never. Ever
Spilled or spoilt. the page —

that I want to be always
                                        be there
 in my journal. no
Not wanting everything and everyone. to be
 re-written

I want to accept
the words
in my mind to be of
importance because this is me
They are mine
And I should be able
to love my words
I should be able to love

my life consists of many things and what I feel about them. étude

My life. consists of boundaries established by the sight angle of
my eyes
As I restrict my vision to minimum
In the minimal emotions should I survive
But. do I live do I. feel the emotions to its full. potential without
being blinded by the trembling feeling of my arms of my wrists I
find that life is not manageable when I look far. away into the
fields the dry blurry vision feels like pain in my eyes and my
heart and. it may seem manageable though I restrict my sight to
a single minimum to a single point of interest at one single
point of time I restrict my feelings to minimal output on my
heart because I am scared of maximums scared of maximizing
the anxiety that may take me to the next level of being not very
young why do I. stop feeling and setting. boundaries
is my answer
to age and anxieties in my life and my answer to dealing with
minimums
how and why do I
it does not matter much. I
just stop. though life continues train drives meetings happen
regularly I rotate around myself I am cold and scared to open
the boundaries.
Broken

war started on 24.02 and I ordered few books étude

I ordered 5 books from Ukrainian bookshop and entered my hometown address on the website - for my mother and sister. I spent few days thinking about which books to order - one of them was a biography of Angela Merkel, another Sally Rooney - for my sister.

The books have never arrived because the post office

was bombed by russia

étude about the X day of war

It has been the X day of war –
she eats those chocolate –
one single piece
ever since –
however tasty Europe might taste –
but freedom in your own land
is sweeter

ich bin und was bin ich nicht étude

Ich bin angekommen
When I saw unfriendly face. for the first time
Ich bin angekommen
When she treated me badly because of my Eastern-European
accent. Many times
Ich bin angekommen
When they said it is important to integrate— there is no other
way —
not even through switching off the subtitles on You Tube. 8 year
ago
Ich bin angekommen
When I killed my previous authentic self and replaced it with
new needs and looks to suit
my current national identity
unverbindlich

Ich bin angekommen
There was another person telling me what language is better
suitable for which occasion
Again

Ich bin angekommen
Things are not done here the way they are done there.
geographically

Ich bin angekommen
Another person asked me where I am from instead of
Who am I / What I am Like

Ich bin angekommen
Ich bin angekommen
Ich bin angekommen

Who will meet who will greet
Me to make the landing softer
Though it may be too late now
Ich bin angekommen —
It is a romance
It is a detective
It is a phantasy

And I am the main character in each story
Every single day

Ich bin angekommen

German museum painting étude

Against dark blue background
Against the walls
Time and space
Collapse inside the golden frames
Within its borders
Lightens up the face of a duke
Or some Dutch duchess
Veronica Spinola Serra
And visible are their hands
Visible are their looks
Not the robes
Maria Giovanna Serra touches
The little hand of her niece
to show the belonging
— this girl belongs to her
like these paintings don't belong to their master
no more

nectareous étude

Sweet thing — this freedom
Nectarous present from above
Eat it
Drink it
Watch it
Take it
Bake it
Finally see it and don't give it

— away

antiquated étude

Metro station entrance and exit
Meet a homeless man
looking for joy to enjoy
Antiquated Christmas music tunes
Lately
They don't bring memories
To the lost souls
Antiquated Christmas music
Antiquated Christmas trees
Are sign of Happy End on Netflix movies
From overseas

however is. étude

However is my second guess
However I am
However all is fine
However I'll never know
Why do I
Feel so stressed

harmony étude

She wanted to walk to see to touch to evolve into something connectable, not the overly superficial being, but the real being with feelings — she wanted above all to be part of things — she was afraid to be - no - no - she didn't know that to be human is not about walking touching evolving into something connectable —humans are disconnected — it is the harmony of mutual suffering that on the upper galactic surface connects us together.
She lost her ability to

start and end of january étude

January doesn't end easy
I wish January
                 would not exist
                 would not possess people

        I wish I could present
        someone May

January doesn't
                      end
                          easy.
Soon we will
                Escape whithersoever
                to the place without selves.

emotionless we will scroll
                down the screen. We will
                shoot the days of bliss

documenting their death
                with high resolution and
                low spirits.

January goes in circles.
                it doesn't end easy
it inhales heavy, loud
it exhales grey, huge
clouds

January requires filters and smiles and day-dreams
overabundance of feelings connected to joy
                              or one single fairy-tale
                              about magic in winter

January is a whale
                              frozen in the empty lake

                                        with no name
                                        with no water

          many visits

          thousand tourists
                              end up pretending to enjoy
                              apocalyptic scenery
                              apocalyptic beautiful future

January doesn't end
                              easy whirlwind I feel
                                        under the skin
                                                  I remind
myself over

                              and
over

every single January day
soon it ends
soon is May

Chapter: 12

12 Études written in Ukrainian language and auto-translated to English with minor improvements from the author

étude to the vineyards

Vineyards
Vineyards and freedom
Far away from home
Fields
Green
As If covered with paper
Innocent people crawl
Discontent

With freedom
So close to the mountains
And the vineyard reminds of the taste

                          in the distance

of being far-away
In Ukraine
So close to sorrow
Far
From home

            in centuries

                 of bondage

етюд про
ВИННІ ПОЛЯ

Винні поля і воля
Далеко від дому
Поля
зеленим
ніби папером покриті
Невинні повзають люди
Невдоволені
Волею
Так близько гори
І винне поле вдалечині
            нагадує смак
Далечі
В Україні
Так близько горе
Далеко
        дому
    в століттях
            поневолених

étude to the sufferer or the sufferess

I wander through the sky without a guide,
And the gray clouds rustle louder and louder
Over gray apartment-blocks
In my memories, is it a sign?
It's a reflection of the swamp, the Polissya,
In the genes of my generation.
It's echoes of bombing sounds,
Of many power plants.
And I am neither a sufferer nor a suffereress.
I'm a wanderer or a wanderess
The sufferer lives near the downtown stations of Kyiv
While I, who knows since when, left the borderlands of suffering.
Only the cranberry, only it,
(I still have to search for its meaning in Wikipedia)
And aimlessly I search for you in the clouds and signs.
My person is like a cranberry
Barely bending under the pressure of its own weight
But not a single gram falls down
Where is my home? From now on
We are all cranberries of suffering,
But not me
I'm in my gray thoughts
Where the gray sky is,
Where there's news about power plants
City centers
Borderlands
Rented flats and
Closeness
If not my closeness with you
Then your closeness
To cloudy news.

ЕТЮД СТРАДНИКУ ЧИ СТРАДНИЦІ

Спроквола блукаю у блакить
і дедалі палахкотіють сірі хмари
у моїх спогадах, чи не знак?
То відзеркалення болота, Полісся
у генах моєї генерації
То відгуки, звуків бомбардування
багатьох електростанцій.

І я не страдник і не страдниця
Я блукач чи блудниця
Страдник живе поряд станцій середмістя
            Києва
Лише журавлина
Лише вока...
(Досі мушу у вікіпедії шукати значення)
і спроквола шукаю у хмарах
тебе і знак

Моя людина — то журавлина
що ледве гнеться
         під тиском власних ваг
але жоден грам не пада додолу

Де ж мій дім?
Відкині
    Бо ми журавлини-страдники
Але не я
Я у сірих думках
Де сіра блакить
Де новини про електростанції
середмістя
     прикордоння
         орендоване житло і
                  близькість
Якщо не мою з тобою
То твою близькість
            до ХМАРНИХ НОВИН

43

sweaty étude

Sweaty études have emerged,
From the music's captivating surge,
We are little too late
In Zhadan's songs, irony is born.
      but what have you done,
           when things were not easy, but undone?
              what did your fear perform,
                  when the time came to move
              on, to transform? What have –

I done
Irony is built on words
And meaning is hidden in sounds
I draw a transparent line
Between
is it études or just a random no-rhyme
I conduct a secret orgy
from songs, from irony in his songs
from the cacophony of the native language sounds
from the euphoria of identical thoughts
identical blood
and shared DNA cells
Completely identical people
Dressed in authentic Carpathian sleeveless jackets
And their completely authentic Ukrainian curses
And so, yes, my études, sweat
from the greatness of all ordinary people
somewhere in a Munich rock hall
somewhere in an abandoned fire station location
my next station
melancholic madness—
and missing home
my next station —ironic
the power of music
not far away from my native road
right here
abroad

СПІТНІЛІ ЕТЮДИ

СПІТНІЛИ ЕТЮДИ
СПІТНІЛИ ЕТЮДИ ВІД МУЗИКИ
СПІЗНИЛИСЯ МИ
В ПІСНЯХ ЖАДАНА ІРОНІЯ
А ЩО ЗРОБИВ ТИ?
     а ЩО ЗРОБИВ ТИ
     КОЛИ ВСЕ НЕ ПРОСТО
     а ЩО ЗРОБИВ СТРАХ
     КОЛИ ЧАС НАСТАВ ЇХАТИ
     ЩО ЗРОБИВ —
Я
НА СЛОВАХ ІРОНІЯ БУДУЄТЬСЯ
А У ЗВУКАХ СХОВАНИЙ ЗМІСТ
     Я ПРОВОДЖУ ПРОЗОРУ ЛІНІЮ
     ПОМІЖ ЕТЮД ЦЕ ЧИ ВІРШ
Я ПРОВОДЖУ СЕКРЕТНУ ОРГІЮ
     ВІД ПІСЕНЬ ВІД ІРОНІЙ В СЛОВАХ
     ВІД КАКОФОНІЇ РІДНОЇ МОВИ
     ВІД ЕЙФОРІЇ ІДЕНТИЧНИХ ДУМОК
     ІДЕНТИЧНОЇ КРОВІ
        і СПІЛЬНИХ ДНК-ових КЛІТИН
ВСЕБІЧНО-ІДЕНТИЧНИХ ЛЮДЕЙ
     ОДЯГНЕНИХ В АВТЕНТИЧНИЙ ПІДЖАК
     ТА ЇХ ВСЕБІЧНО-АВТЕНТИЧНИХ
        УКРАЇНСЬКИХ МАТІВ
і ПОТІЮТЬ МОЇ ЕТЮДИ —
ВІД ВЕЛИЧІ ПРОСТИХ ЛЮДЕЙ
     ДЕСЬ У МЮНХЕНСЬКОМУ РОК-ЗАЛІ
     ДЕСЬ НА ПОКИНУТІЙ ПОЖЕЖНІЙ ІНСТАНЦІЇ
МОЯ НАСТУПНА СТАНЦІЯ
СУМ —   ЗА ДОМОМ
МОЯ НАСТУПНА —   ІРОНІЯ
     СИЛА МУЗИКИ
        НЕ ДАЛЕКО
           ТУТ ЗА КОРДОНОМ

étude to my thoughts

My thoughts
Burdened by imagination
By decaying little cloud
Sorrow doesn't let go
Only calm rushes out of me
Like rain, it waterfalls on the grass
On the greenish, on the asphalt, on the ashes
Of scattered cigarettes

My thoughts are structured
With and without mood
Divided into two halves
Which one do I choose
Like clothing
Today
Which one do I choose
Like a conception
Like an artist
        like a canvas

ЕТЮД МОЇМ ДУМКАМ

мої думки
замарскі уявою
образою хмариною
журба не помилне
лише спокій рекуб
як доц — уназ та траву
на зелень, на асфальт, на попіл
розсипаних цигарок

мої думки структуровані
без настрою і з настроєм
подібні на дві половинки
яку обираю я
як одяг
сьогодні
яку вибираю я
як вибір
як мистецтво
як канвас

home away from home étude

While riding on the subway train, I glanced for a moment out the window – because other moments I spent contemplating the life of the Linkin Park band's lead singer on subway trains – what is happening in the big world out there? – and there, it was all dark blue - a porous little cloud hovered over the roofs of the industrial district of Bad-Cannstatt: with cranes of construction structures for cemented tunnels and metal bridges – forcefully hanging inadvertently over the wide river, like the Dnipro or the Danube, but dirty like the exhaust fumes of downtown, the Neckar river, which serves only to facilitate the transportation of consumerist goods of the 21st century – back and forth, iron blocks of modern junk float on the ferry. I found myself as if in some polluted 19th-century Scotland, where gangsters in movies carry weapons and wear peaky blinders caps – because like them – my cap is this deceptive dark blue of a foggy cloud – and no matter where my subway train goes, no matter where my boat sails – the cargo remains the same – and like that barge, I have to drag it along with me everywhere.

ДІМ ДАЛЕКО ВІД ДОМУ ЕТЮД

Їдучи у поїзді метро, я глянула на мить у вікно — адже інші миті я проводила роздумуючи про життя соліста Лінкін Парк у поїздах метро — що ж там робиться у великому світі? — А там все темно-синьо — пориста хмаринка, повисла над дахами індустріального району Бад-Канштатт: з кранами будових конструкцій цементованих тунелей та металевих мостів — силоміць нависла ненароком накоротко над широкою, як Дніпро, чи як Дунай, але брудною (як вихлопи середмістя) річкою Некар, яка слугує лише для полегшення вантажних перевозів консюмеристського покупця 21-го століття — туди-сюди плавають залізні блоки модерного брухту на поромі. Попала я, ніби у якусь забруднену викидами фабрик, Шотландію 19-го століття, де у фільмах гангстери носять зброю і шапку-картуз — бо як і воинций мій картуз — це опаклива темно-синя блакить сірої хмари — і куди не поїде мій поїзд метро, куди не попливе мій пліт — вантаж залишається той самий — і я, як та баржа, мушу його за собою повсюди тягати.

summer étude

What does summer feel?
What do I feel
When I gaze into the park
The museum path and the grey statue
Is it possible that I lack

The sense of sequence?

Етюд про літо

Що відчуває літо
що відчуваю я
коли вдивляюся у парк
доріжка музей і статуя
                сіра
невже у мене нема
                відчуття
послідовності

running away étude

I escape into myself
From myself
And even here, I am not close by

People run away from themselves
People run away
Everywhere

The water flows

ВТІКАЮЧИ ~~ЕТЮД~~

ВТІКАЮ У СЕБЕ
ВІД СЕБЕ
А ТАМ МЕНЕ ТЕЖ НЕМА

ТІКАЮТЬ ЛЮДИ ВІД СЕБЕ
ТІКАЮТЬ ЛЮДИ
ВСЮДИ

ТЕЧЕ ВОДА

numbness étude

Desires have become numb
Grief awakens inside the body
Divide me with a dot
A coma
A semicolon

I gaze into the distance
Blindness
To reach the end
Movement is necessary
Feelings frozen
From exhaustion
Spring has ended
That's all

There is no
Connection with tomorrow

ЕТЮД ОНІМІННЯ

ОНІМІЛИ БАЖАННЯ
ОЖИВАЄ СУМ
        ВСЕРЕДИНІ ТІЛА
ВІДДІЛИЛИ МЕНЕ КРАПКОЮ
КОМОЮ
SEMIKOLON

ГЛЯНУ ВДАЛЬ
СЛІПОТА
ЩОБ ДІСТАТИСЯ КІНЦЯ
ТРЕБА РУХАТИСЬ
ЗАВМЕРЛИ ПОЧУТТЯ
ВІД ВТОМИ

УСЕ.
ЗАКІНЧИЛАСЬ ВЕСНА

ІЗ ЗАВТРА НЕМАЄ
ОБ'ЯЗКУ

This is not auto-generated not-an-étude "Humanoid KA"

Humanoid KA has committed a serious offense; they have been infected with the virus "war" for a year, but nobody knows about it. Nowadays, war is a virus more contagious than Corona, more frightening than the fear of vaccinations, more bizarre than belief in UFOs.

For a long time, war has been a part of them, but they were not a part of war; they secretly tried to resist, not showing their symptoms to anyone.

They attempted to fight the war, but their equipment was insufficient. What does one actually need as a war-infected? Their first thought was to open a ticket at the Infected-by-War-Consulting:

"Infection alert. Symptoms: chaotic thinking, conflict between reason and emotion that throws me into a sudden loss of control. Assign someone to me."

The assigned war consultant arrived immediately and found a body on the floor that seemed ill-equipped for war.

"The virus is transmitted through the war-ratio radio. How can someone be so affected by it? We will search their AI mind for sources of problems."

> *"Bomb! Fire! Help! We are okay, are you? Help! Are you there? Fleeing bodies, Come, camp, boxes, pack, send, are you there? I am not well. Are you there? Doctor? Are you there? Appointments in a few months? Are you there? Pain,are you there? Therapist? You there? Doctor? Anyone?"*

Now our war consultant (Johnny) knew: Humanoid KA's AI mind had been damaged. Repairing it would be the task of a technician, not Johnny's problem.

Case "war-damaged #2402" - CLOSED, Johnny wrote in his online report.

The paralyzed KA was removed, life went on, UFOs continued to orbit the Earth, Corona continued to circulate, and no, no, they still hadn't experienced war, but the war still raged outside of them.

I wish I could close this chapter, or someone? Anyone?

"Are you there?"

Це не авто-згенерований не етюд «Humanoid КА»

Гуманоїд КА вчинила важке порушення правил, вона заражена вірусом під назвою "війна" протягом року, але ніхто про це не знає.

Сьогодні війна - це вірус, що швидше розповсюджується, ніж корона, що викликає страх, більший, ніж страх перед щепленнями, і що більш дивний, ніж віра в НЛО.

Війна була частиною її життя на протязі довгого часу, але вона не була частиною війни, вона таємно намагалася їй протистояти, не показуючи своїх симптомів нікому.

Вона намагалася боротися з війною, але її знаряддя були недостатні. Що насправді потрібно інфікованим фійною? Першою думкою було відкрити квиток у Консультації Інфікованих Війною:

«Увага: можливість інфікування. Симптоми: хаотичне мислення, конфлікт між розумом і почуттями, що зводить мене з ніг з раптовою втратою контролю. Призначте мені когось".

Надісланий військовий консультант з'явився миттєво і знайшов труп на підлозі, який, здається, був недостатньо готовим до війни.

"Вірус передається через військове радіо. Як людина може так постраждати від цього? Ми перевіримо її штучний інтелект на наявність проблем".

> *"Бомба! Вогонь! Допоможіть! Ми в порядку, а ви? Допоможіть! Чи ви там? Тіло, яке втікає, Пакуйте, відправляйте, чи ви там? Мені погано. Ви там?Лікар? Чи ви там? через кілька місяців? Чи ви там? Болить. Чи ви там? Терапевт? Ви там? Лікар? Хтось? Будь-хто?"*

Тепер наш військовий консультант (Джонні) зрозумів: штучний інтелект Humanoid КА був пошкоджений. Його відновлення стане завданням техніка, а не Джонні.

Справу "пошкоджений війною #2402" - ЗАКРИТО, записав Джонні в своєму онлайн-звіті.

Паралізовану КА забрали, життя продовжувалося, НЛО продовжували обертатися навколо Землі, корона продовжувала своє існування, і ні, ні, Гуманоїд КА досі не перехворіла на вірус «війна» - але війна продовжувала відбуватися поза нею.

Я бажав би завершити цей розділ, або хтось? Будь-хто?
"Ви там?"

étude to Ukrainian museum painting

I long to have

red
When all around is gray
Buildings and walls
I long to have -
Burning with desires
Blushing and dreaming of
Extraordinary things

I long to have red
When all around is grey
Buildings and walls
I long to have

That greyish sky
Is burning

[етюд картині]
в музеї

так хочеться мати
— червоний
коли навколо сірі
будівлі і стіни
так хочеться мати —

горіти бажаннями
червоніти і мріяти про

неординарне

хочеться мати червоний
коли навколо сірі
будівлі і стіни
хочеться мати

горить
те сіре небо

crossing-the-border étude

I will cross the border –
become someone else
I will cross the border –
step over my own self
I will transition from who I was
Into the person I should be
I will cross the border –
become better

I will cross the border
Change my feathers
What will it be like –
The transformation of my character
Under a dramatic final act
In a film about a phoenix -
Tedious

This is not the end – but the hero dies
I will cross the border
And the film has ended

ЕТІСД ПРО ПЕРЕХІД КОРДОНУ

Перейду кордон —
стану іншою
Перейду кордон —
Переступлю через своє я
Перейду із того якою була
в особистість якою мала би
буде

Перейду кордон —
стану кращою
перейду кордон
переодягну пір'я
яке ж бого —
переродження мого персонажу
під драматичний фінальний
кінець

у фільмі про фенікс —
нудне
це не кінець — але герои помирає
перейду кордон
і закінчився фільм

étude to my hometown Lutsk

In the city of entertainment,
And by sorrow filled shopping centers,
The clouds and mist have frozen forever,
Figures hidden behind big prices
breathe,
Inhale —

In the midst of Warsaw market
Or somewhere in the department store
Shoppers burdened with bags
Carry their sale purchases home
And in the pile, they hold back thoughts
About the gloomy weather.

Together with the crowd,
They head from one
Shopping center
To a restaurant, to forget
The cloudy weather,
And later,
To Tam-Tam
And then the mist will dissolve,

This is how they learned
to indulge themselves —
By sorrow.

January 2022

Етюд мого рідного міста

У місті розваг
І наповнених сумом торгових центрів
Застигли навічно хмара і пара
Затьмарені цінами постаті дихають
В ди — х

Посеред варшавського ринку
Або десь у ЦУМі
Скуті пакетами покупці
Несуть додому розпродажі
І у купі стримають думки
Про політику і погану погоду

Укупі всі разом
Прямують з одного центру
Торгового
В ресторан, щоб забути
Хмарну погоду
А згодом
В там-там
І пара розвівається
Балувати себе навчилися —
Сумом

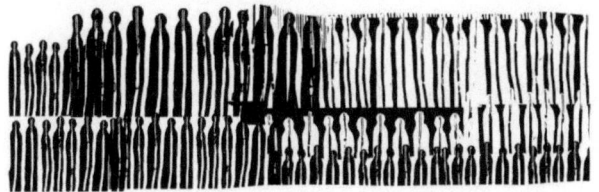

Chapter: 2020

The content of the chapter 2020 is self-obvious

love étude

Unsent message to God:
Life is it real
Is it
I dream in years
I
Am I
Love is it timeless
Why
Do I love
Why do you stop
Loving
Why do you love

étude about continuing the thought of the previous author

From "Breaking [News]" by Noor Hindi
„We´ll wake up, Sunday morning, and read the paper. Read each other. Become"…

Cockroaches after reading Kafka
Or we´ll become stanzas from Rilke
Or we´ll become sy-lla-bles
in complicated poems
Hopelessly written by unknown writers
Punished by creative society

Writers
who only dream
Of getting published
In books
In newspapers
In magazines
Writers who are recognized
Only in the hidden notebooks
Left on shelves
to dust
Forgotten poems about unknown
Will be there
Typed
In BOLD
We will wake up on Sunday
And all the papers
Will be sold out
And all those writers
Will be known
And a little bit spoiled

prolixity is étude

"a tendency to speak or write at great or tedious length, long-windedness"

Would you stop talking
Would you silence the crowd
The prolixity of thinking
Exceeds the written down
Books
written thoughts
instantaneous action
Takes over the debate
I look around the crowd

Do you belong there?
A part
Of the party
A party started live
Transmission on television

the ideology is set
On the world's stage
Don't judge it
It has just started
To perform the reform
to entertain the audience
With a taste for certain
Twists tweets
And a few likes
Given to violence

summer étude written in winter

It's just like winter never happened that girl is wearing open
sandals
I am still dressed in winter
And I ask
What have I done
I also deserve sun,

do I

the bitterness of the ephemeral étude

bit
by bit
the bitterness
on the platform
in front of the train ride
going away is hard
for no reason
she cries
this is the moment

this is good-bye

I close my eyes
I see her now

bit by bit
disappearing
away into
blurry January
Bloody February
That last moment
I see her
Bit by bit the bitterness
On the platform
      Forever she is
      Waiting
I am waiting
Forever in the ephemeral

contemporary love étude

What´s not to love about
A single tree
In the middle

What´s not to love about
A plain field
Empty

Of any meaning

What´s not to love
About
Silence

As long as it is there
As long as
Silent

What´s not to love about
A single leave
Falling

What´s not to love about winter autumn
What´s not to love about
A single tree
On the empty plain field

At home

étude to being independent. forever

When my friend said not to worry
One day we all will meet
And be free

And continuous

I felt helplessly ridiculous
Inside of the cages of circumstances

Nothing is free
Neither you
Nor me

summer étude about feeling overwhelmed by the recent events

July is over and there´s very little
Emotion

Deep inside me left
Theft happened and

Who is to blame –
Who asks –
Who knows –
Who stays honnest to their selves
With their feelings nowadays
All is different –
All is fine –
Good morning good evening
Don´t you mind –

A little don't care in July
A little emotionless winter
And summer –
And a very over the top
Spring –
Happened to everyone
and to me –
I wish it to be finally
 O v e r
But this July
Continues the spring
And I continue

To blame emptiness
Inside of me
For the heat
In the middle of winter-ness.

étude to trying and failing

Poem   about   trying   —

I   am.

Poem   about   failing   —

am I?

étude to her blue jeans

I´ve left my favourite pair
pair of blue jeans
you might wonder
– where –
on the old sofa
at your place

so you might have to
wear them
on a rainy day
so you might remember
the smell
of my hair
and then
I´ll rememeber –
I´ll remember you then

étude to having. breakfast

we ate some noodles for _____
to break the routine
tasks
did I know that
this memory would last
of you and me
and a cheap taste
talking through the morning
about future day-deals
so fast
did I take a moment
to notice how you talk
how you pause

_____

in a meadow of
thoughts was I
so no
didn´t notice
until coffee arrived

étude to the process of listening to the. radio

in the rooms a chatter gets
louder
even though nobody listens
to the radio
anymore
even though
much more
it has been ever since
six months after the last
christmas
happiness has never come
had never
to existence
and we´re all a global witness
of
a non-existing crime of our time
commited by –

the break into our schedule
creates some space
silence was totally undervalued
over –
though we don't believe in –
now everybody listens to the
radio

étude to having. blank spaces. and hope

i´ve named it _____
though you may give it many names
to the handwritten list
of psychological horror
bly manor
adventure-drama-monogamy
up-to-mood comedy
black-mirror director´s cut
upload

I´ve named it _____
I´ve seen it end
so please don´t judge
my life on screen
I´ve missed to live
but not to list
so I have had a _____

étude to the love of the colour. blue

dear friend, of the universe
I envy you. you see
the world upside down
or perhaps it isn´t you but me.
I see in every you the colour. blue
deep shades of sad
joy-full-ness sleep in-
side me or you when
we´re in bed. waiting
for sunrise to eat
the mood. for breakfast
are served epitomes of
style-full readings
of poetry
made from you and
from being without you. emptied
in your eyes
I am without. sense
thrown into universe with
the desire to invent
something inside us
that was not supposed to
go though

but I try. I write
the sense into the world
without purpose
to recreate that
poem-mood. what

nobody has but I
desire with
every you
       the color comes
       into my mind – .

lovely étude to my. sister

the she
I met her once
      and forever
I met her –
      is it love
I met her
      I see her
today tomorrow

yesterday
is being all about
her

why does it matter
      why do I buy that
      christmas sweater
      times two
why I write the letters
      without telling her
      that this is she
      the one who
          matters once and forever
I met her –
      is it love

neighbours this étude is for you

I see no light
the cat must
have gone to eat
to sleep to reinvent
the light itself with it´s laziness
I see just dark spotlight of
november-ness
without leaves
just barren trees
I see the life
in front of my window
not mine to judge
not mine to touch
I see no light
no cat
it´s just dark-ness

december comes and all will change étude

flawsome personalities
are hard to un-cover —
behind each
is an act
of pretense
a hidden story
a memory
forbidden agony
in the heart
intensive break point
or someone who
has constantly being
annoyed by gloom

so the promise was
to change
to alter —
not themselves
though the attitudes

dreamy étude to chaos of the mind

in a dream
the bus. did not take
me. to the art
university. instead
it took me home
to look at the blurred
representation of
your personality

in a dark-obsessed
dream-light
I see a sight a glimps
of your eyes
in vein —

an amorist am I
adventurous to visit
the art —

instead I felt the pain
of watching you
with no moral quality
a simple feel and go
a simple ache
to loose a way
home
to lose the sense of time
of life

I did not make it to the
university

though I woke up
indeed I did

étude to music

the music volume
is up loud
to interfere with essence
of my real thoughts
to paralyze myself
to stop the flow
to kill with the beat
the honest feel
of being
down

slow down

leave yourself out
out of your head
dive ahead
to the next track

having a nightmare is like. étude

every day as a rebel
not quite asleep
awake
inactive
victim of a day
I think I lay
I may have
even thought about you
once —
the second time I scream
I've seen you leave
was just in a dream.

to quiescent reality
I open my eyes
it makes me inert
motionless
paralyzed sad

though I rebel
I scream
in turns
when I sleep

étude to postmodern Christmas

Coca-Cola – he is near
life is busy when you leave in a hurry
sticky traces on McDonald's floor
life is not life anymore
when you notice
together with traces you left yourself
there in McDonald's
there on the floor
together with your shoe laces
you stuck right in front of the waiting line
and you walk on and on and you try to run
you try on the new shoes on and on
but nothing feels like like those old ones

stuck there somewhere behind you on the sticky floor
and you don't notice this loss
until you find yourself in the middle of a big misunderstanding
of having it all but owning nothing so you run back barefoot to
that moment to that floor when having nothing meant having it
all because dreams don't stick to anything they are flying free
flying high abstract unshaped

but I lost my dreams when I entered the shop when I ordered
'to go' I lost it all being in a hurry I lost my dreams on the go I
lost myself in a hurry I didn't notice when my shoe laces did not
belong to my shoes anymore I didn't notice my life went
shopping to buy a new version of myself.

what taking-a-pill-feels-like étude

I took a pill
nobody wished
a happy Monday
I took a pill
I am ill from watching
TV – – –

I've mistaken TV
for reality –
I took a pill
out of curiosity –
I took a pill
it is Monday
because nobody will
wish a merry – – –

I took a pill
before Christmas –
I took a pill
one
not too much
one is not enough
on such brutal morning
such brumal Monday mood

I took the claire de lune pill
to vomit the news
from the last weekend
it spreads inside

my body's weak
it spreads it goes it does not stop
going viral

I took a pill
Mondays are not the future
Mondays are male
Mondays are pale
I took a pill against winter days
I took a pill to have Friday fun
I turned grey
into pale green

I took a pill
to remember how from feeling mad
I may be feeling overly
entertained by boredom

étude full of complex verbs

I wrote I read
eidetic poetics
to angelify the thread
of my feeling
mad
scrolling down
long lines of virtual
life
to heavenize
the cold wind
blowing digital leaves
further and further away
from digital trees
it´s real
real winter
I see in the window
through the glass

étude to a homeless in Augsburg

it will be never the same as it is now, the leaves are falling, the days are crawling – away. what do I know about walking, perhaps about scrolling down to see more and more but not to feel, the feelings have fallen into the past tense. have you seen present? I haven´t seen anything in days except for I love the falling, the crawling, the scrolling – not through the memories, but through the past. and when I was walking and fading away into then and now, I saw drifting far away in the day-light-dark, a blurred concept of a person drifting and drifting away, apart. I was interested why? I walked behind and wondered why – why the smell – why the bags – why she was not in a hurry. while she walked, I walked, behind her and then she turned – left. she carried a luggage of life, of days and I carried something similar though I could let it go, I could throw it away – I could leave it behind in a park, in the snow, I could hide it away. her luggage though was real, real bags with real names of people who let her down, perhaps even let her go, outside, into the autumn, left her alone in a cold. though she wasn´t lost, she headed forward partly as some foreigner, partly as she had an aim. then she turned, to the bench hidden away from society, hidden within the orange bushes and yellow trees and I distanced myself from her, it was the distance of two different lives, one full of dreams, another full of staff, though which is who I could not tell. until now.

étude divided in.appropriate.dots

the flowers
on the market are too
expensive, so I buy
them in a supermarket,
that's why I can afford two
bouquets of different
colors. why would one
color be. not. enough?
even though most flowers
like most souls die
without natural surroundings,
mine is/are alive
in the sight of newly acquired
entities. business. the package
shows two men —
the owners,
who supposedly own
this flower-business
for few centuries
now. how soul.less.is it?
to own something
so dead that makes one feel so a.
life. I'd prefer
the field full of artifacts
of similar to original
flower breeds —
to gather them, cut
the strong stems
from below the ground.

supposedly it is a great
idea, it does even exist,
but life is too busy
for ideas, for people, for plants.
so busy you don't even
notice the fall. of the.
leaves. would you stay?
how slowly your newly-bought

flowers are. alive?

étude to not going often enough to the old library in Augsburg

I´ve never been inside. the library
architectural memory
of a great designer
who happened to live
somewhere around
who happened to have
it all structural
in the imagination
who happed to live here
who constructed the walls
the doors the huge windows
and the huge stairs. the books?

they were partly designed too
after they had been written
not by a designer
but by the writers who
perhaps did not think
of them as writers at all −
merely sharing memories
of knowledge. were there also
female? writers? back then!
writers were and writers are −
designed! no, not at the local
ancient library, at the modern
local store! sounds like a drama.

theater? is under construction.

though library keeps its doors open –
gorgeously. old. the writing
keeps flowing, but people keep staying –
at their homes. the book temple
of this circle of buyers/lovers
is around the corner –
simple merchandise – a book chain,
which satisfies their consumers´ desires,
lending books have never been
so out of date! today.

it is the pure design
and not of the stores, it is
about book covers
and the target. fashion. the library-designer did not mean to
threaten –
a very local chain-bookstore
in the future,
so it stays empty.
the library. with its collection
of antique scripts. the society
prefers to own rather than
to borrow, the books –
as if they own the life, as if
they borrow – and le(nd)t.
it. go.

étude to depilation epilator elevators

Depilation epilator elevator trends
French trench-coat
random rainbows
Rhythmic melodic slow fast-forwarded
Moving backwards
Explaining mansplaining spreading
Reading the booking-reviewing madness
— no hair
or sense of an epilogue
in my love to life

étude to a pfefferbretzel

A pretzel can be with salt and butter
A pretzel can be hard
Though a pretzel with pepper
Is my life

epilogue

Even though there is no point in anything, I seek to give a narrative to life and this is a study based on numbers connected to feelings, perhaps you ask yourself how it is possible? Giving narratives is not easy, especially if philosophy could not, perhaps you can?

Table of contents:

acknowledgements étude

Limitless inspiration of writing this book of études came from a tiny greyish book that I received.

Just imagine: there we are with Simon Keim, in the old baroque-styled apartment, ceiling decorated with ornaments, on the 5th floor, the table is full with food and left-overs, champagne, and small colourful lights hanging on the balcony where as few as 6 people have gathered around, dressed in glitter, glitter is even spread on the faces, sounds coming from huge piano playing from the living room – the New Year´s Eve in Kyiv – 31st of December 2021, and among the wishes of the president Zelenskyj on the not-that-old TV-set in Kirtoka´s apartment, I vividly remember her friend from Donetsk crying – then, I receive, covered in handcrafted paper, self-made ceramic plate that can be used for candles with a hand-painted handshake on it from Oksana Ginchuk, and this – tiny *poesie* collection, an original print with yellowish pages published in 1962 by Ivan Drach called "Sunflowers". That New Year has changed everything – thank you Kirtoka and the girl from Donetsk for staying strong, thank you Oksana Ginchuk for your art-for-donation that saves people, thank you Simon for being there through each étude for the past months and for your editing – you are quite an artist yourself.

I would not make this book ready in time without Stuttgart Writing Circle of girls: thank you for your no-criticism-at-all and pro-postmodernist feedback – Eva, Charlie and Jane. You continue to inspire me. I wish we can keep writing every two weeks forever.

Also, Frank Keim who through persistence and huge experience in scientific publishing has always motivated me to continue my creative flow, and especially your huge help with blank pages – all the blanks in this book are thanks to you!

Last but not least, thank you my sister Liza for another book-cover that does attain undivided Ukrainian nostalgic presence with the first look, I hope that your studies will bring even more courage into your creative process and inspire you to great beginnings in life.

And to my mother *(дякую мамі)* – thank you for reading *"Kateryna"* to me every day when I was 5, so I could learn it by heart, before I learned to read.

practice example

This book is celebrating the ancient Ukrainian technique of writing études. However, without your input, we cannot spread the beloved tradition further, so here is space for you to practice and to become your own writer and somewhat painter.

1.   So, what's your object of desire (ood)?
Peanut butter

2.   Define your ood:
More than just a food cream, even if I am not an American, it gives me a solid protein foundation for my every day

3.   With what words, feelings, signs do you associate your ood?
Jelly, mostly dark German bread, sweetness, escapism, strength

4.   Compare your ood with other things going through your mind?
Peanut butter is a strong breakfast ingredient providing energy to the house of my body, like an offshore wind-park provides to a country

5.   What is your ood made of?
Crunchy ingredients, power, love

6.   With what colours do you associate your ood with?
The colour of a new day, so maybe yellow-orange?

7.   What speaks in favour and against your ood?
In favour: Energy and comfort provider
Against: It could have a more optimistic colour and appearance

Congratulations on making it thus far! Please now combine all gathered étude elements for your final piece of work.

Etude to the flow of the morning

Dark morning, heavy, hectic thoughts
Dark German bread, sweetness, escape is what I long for
Crunchy ingredients, power, love, felt taste after taste
Energy and comfort
Vigor to begin a new day

Practice by: Simon Keim

practice space